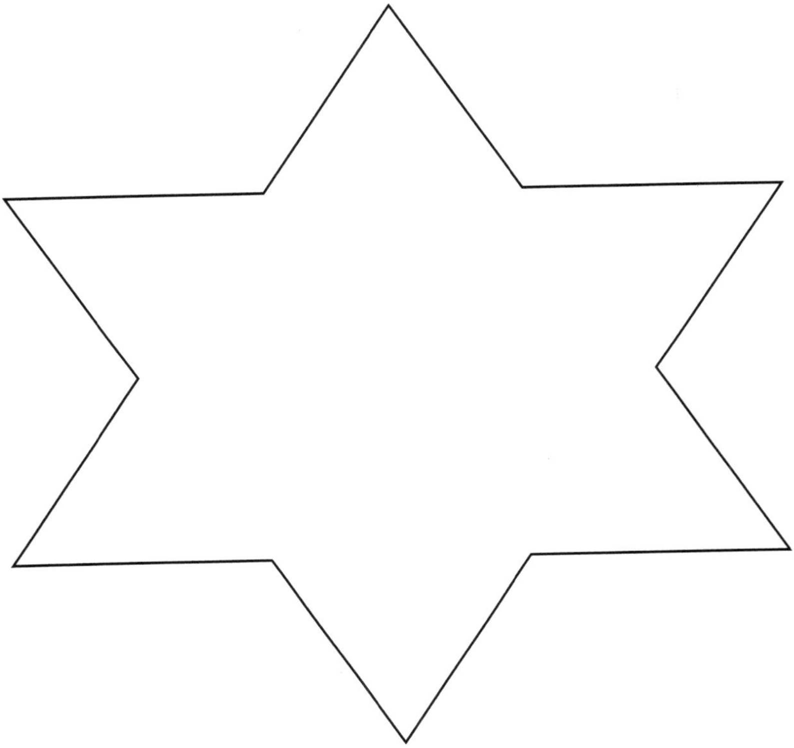

Please Read this First

This is a daily blank lined writing notebook for those of use in recovery from substance misuse and addiction to addictive behaviors.

How It Works:
There are many ways of using this notebook. Three main ways of using this notebook are:

1. Use this book as a prompt journal. Each page has a prompt question that you can use every day for your personal recovery.

2. Use this book as a personal writing notebook that you can use to take meeting notes, school notes, doodle, draw, and do whatever else you want.

3. See the prompt questions on each page and think about or meditate on the question and carry on with your day to day activities.

This is a lined writing notebook strategically designed for those of us in recovery from substance misuse and behavioral addictions. You may use this book as a systematic method for organizing and formatting your recovery notes, study notes and your personal recovery practice.

If you are an addictions counselor, therapist or recovery coach, and you have clients and or students whose recovery and healing you are supporting, this can be a notebook to keep track of your sessions, keep track or their recovery and healing progress and most importantly, keep track of your own progress as a helper.

Describe what and or who you are grateful for today.

Which of your gifts are you not fully utilizing?

On a scale of 1 – 10, how perfect is your life?

How might your past successes get in your way?

Describe a nice moment spent with family or friends in the past week.

How have you changed the world for generations to come?

Describe any actions that if you took, could change everything.

Describe something interesting that happened today.

Describe something good that happened to you today.

Describe something beautiful or interesting you saw in the past week.

If you weren’t scared, what would you do?

What was a nice thing someone said to you in the past week?

How has another person shown that they care about you, within the past week?

What could keep you from getting the life you want?

Who do you need to become in order to achieve your new goals?

On a scale of 1 – 10, how honest can you be with your family?

Describe what and or who you are grateful for today.

Describe the best part of your day.

What's the worst that can happen this year, and can you handle that?

Describe what and or who you are grateful for today.

Describe what and or who you are grateful for today.

Describe what and or who you are grateful for today.

If things don't change, how would that affect your life, and who else would be affected?

What would your life look like if you were entirely successful?

Considering your emotional and financial resources, what is possible for you?

Describe something exciting that happened this past week.

Describe what your inner wisdom is saying about your best life

Describe everything that needs to happen for you to change your life.

What rules do you have that are getting in your way?

What will you have to give up in order to make room for your goals?

What are you willing to commit to improve your life?

If a friend were in your shoes, what advice would you give them?

What will your legacy be, what will the fourth generation from now say about you?

Describe what might keep you from becoming who you want to become.

What was something nice you said in the past week?

Describe a challenge you overcame in the past week.

What needs your immediate attention?

Describe something good you did for another person in the past week.

What has contributed to your success so far?

What can you do starting today to get you on track to your best life?

Describe the advantages of your dream.

What goal are you ready to achieve?

On a scale of 1 – 10 how honest have you been to yourself?

Who do you know who can help you with getting better?

What are some steps that you can take this week towards achieving your best life?

Describe how you served others this week.

Describe any ways you could transform your life this week.

Describe the important questions you should be asking yourself.

How did you show someone that you care about them, within the past week?

How will you test your ideas?

If you could have anything, what would you have right now?

Describe what you have learned this week?

How can you improve your life, so it adds value forever?

What is so important to you that you would defend it with your life?

Describe what and or who you are grateful for today.

What are you grateful for this week?

Describe a moment when you felt calm, content, or relaxed today.

Describe how comments about you from other people are slowing you down.

Describe who is taking advantage of you, and what's good about it.

Describe how your current environment support or sabotage who you're becoming.

What are you putting up with, and how is that holding you back?

Describe the dreams you've given up on.

Describe how you made someone else's day better.

Describe something that made you laugh in the past week.

How can you enjoy the process of your personal growth?

Describe what is great about your life this week.

Describe what and or who you are grateful for today.

Describe something you were thankful for today.

What could you be excited about if you chose to be?

Describe any step you take that would make the biggest difference, right now.

Describe something that made you happy today.

Describe why your personal development matters to other people.

What is your most urgent challenge?

Where do you want to be by this time next year?

How can you get your needs fully met?

What are you pretending not to know?

Describe what and or who you are grateful for today.

Describe how someone has helped you in the past week.

What are your biggest mistakes and what did you learn from them?

Describe what your ideal life looks like.

What obstacles have you faced in the past, what did you do, and what did you learn?

Describe something kind you saw another person do in the past week.

Describe something fun you did today.

What would be your next goal after you achieve your current one?

What opportunities are you missing and where are you falling behind?

What are you willing to stop doing to improve your life?

Describe something that made this past week special.

Describe what and or who you are grateful for today.

Describe what and or who you are grateful for today.

Describe your detailed strategy for achieving your goals.

Describe how you are living on your Plan B, instead of your Plan A.

Describe what and or who you are grateful for today.

Describe something you did today that you can be proud of.

Describe what and or who you are grateful for today.

Describe a time when you were happy for someone else in the past week.

Whose life are you really living?

Where do you get your motivation from?

If you woke up with courage, how could your life change?

Describe assumptions that you are making.

Who is or might be counting on you to achieve your goals?

What things do you need to start delegating?

Who might be excited about your successes?

What will really make the biggest difference in your life?

Describe a personal strength you used today.

What can you accomplish this week that doesn't depend on others?

Describe what you accomplished this week.

Describe the biggest challenge you have.

Who do you know who is or might be grateful for you?

What would you be doing right now if you had unlimited resources?

Describe how you could use your past to your advantage.

Describe your strategy for achieving your goals.

Describe how your personal development would help you become more.

What obstacles do you expect to face this week?,
How do you plan to address them?

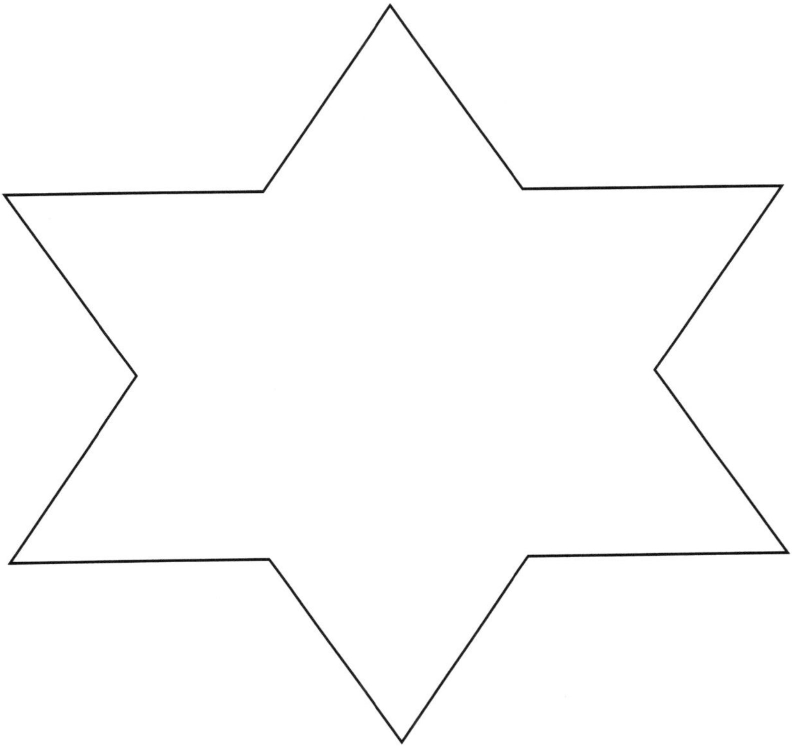

The creator of this writing journal is also available for strategic sober coaching and healing on: TovNation (at) Gmail (dot) com.

Made in the USA
Middletown, DE
24 May 2022

66198762R00066